Embroidery Hoop Christmas Ornaments

Copyright © 2020

DEDICATION

Content

Embroidery Hoops Christmas Farmhouse Style

Supplies Needed:

- embroidery hoops (3" or 4")

- black paint, or dark brown stain

- paintbrush or rag

- scrapbook papers in plaid or music print

- ribbon and/or twine

- holiday greenery

- scissors

- glue stick

- hot glue gun

Embroidery Hoop Christmas Ornaments

How to Make:

Step 1: Loosen the embroidery hoop clasp and separate into two sections. Paint and/or stain the embroidery hoops. painted all front sides and the inner rings. Leave to dry. (This might be a good time to grab a Christmas cookie. Just sayin.')

Embroidery Hoop Christmas Ornaments

Step 2: Using a pencil, trace the outline of your embroidery hoop on the back side of your scrapbook paper. (Male sure you use the larger part of the hoop, the one with the clasp at top).

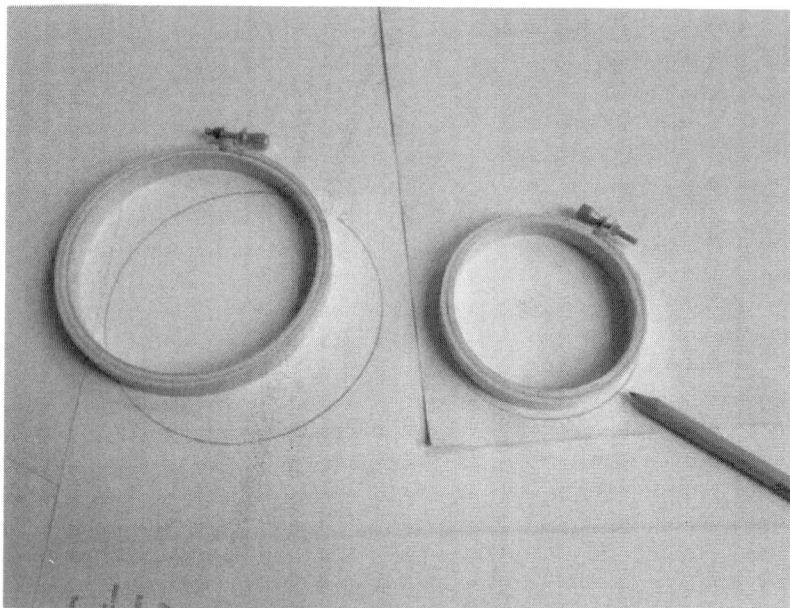

Step 3: Cut the circles out of your scrapbook paper using a scissors.

Step 4: Place the two parts of your embroidery hoop back together and tighten the clasp so they stay securely together. Apply glue to the back side of your embroidery hoop.

Step 5: With your scrapbook paper flat on your work surface, with the pattern-side facing UP, set your embroidery hoops in place and press down so the glue will stick to the paper. (It's important to see your paper pattern while gluing to the embroidery hoop so that you can center the design as needed.)

Step 6: Cut small sprigs of greenery and arrange together in small clumps. Hot glue pieces together if necessary. (For a couple of my ornaments tied the little arrangement together with a bit of twine. For the others, used hot glue in strategic places to hold the berries and greens together.)

Step 7: Place a line of hot glue on your embroidery hoop, where you want to attach the greens. Quickly press greens in place as glue cools.

Step 8: Cut a length of ribbon or twine approx. 12" long.

Step 9: String the ribbon through the small clasp of the embroidery hoop.

Step 10: Tie the ribbon together at the ends, and you are all set to hang your pretty new ornament on the tree!

Red Plaid Embroidery Hoop Christmas Ornament

SUPPLIES

- Small piece of scrap plaid fabric
- 4" Wood Embroidery Hoop
- DecoArt Acrylic Paint Christmas Red
- E6000 Glue
- Red Glitter Ribbon (Hobby Lobby)
- Christmas Pick (Hobby Lobby)
- Spray Starch

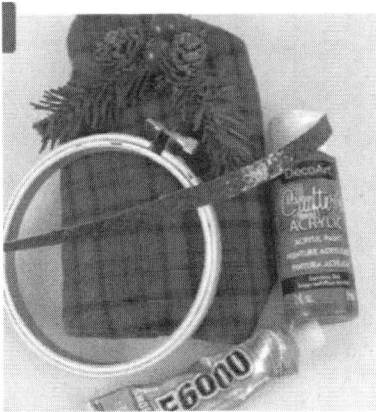

First we paint the wood embroidery hoop.

Paint the inside and outer edges of the small hoop. No need to paint the outside edge as it will be hidden by the fabric. Only paint the outer edges of the large hoop as shown.

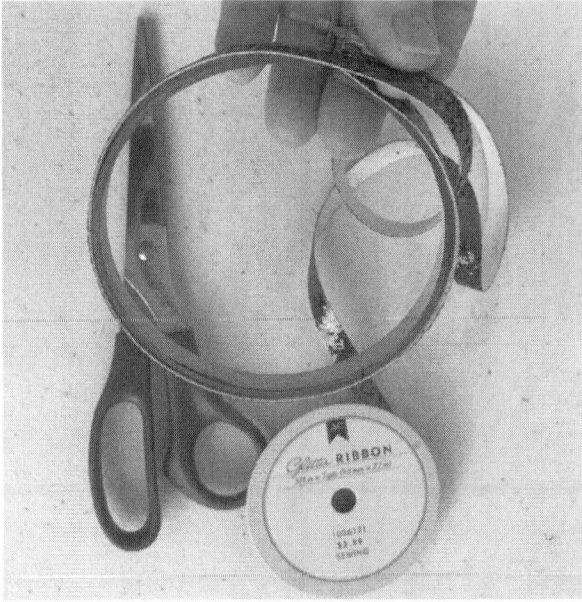

Next measure and cut the glitter ribbon for the outside of the top hoop. Just wrap it around then cut to fit. Set aside while you measure and cut the fabric.

After ironing lay the larger hoop onto the fabric. Using a pencil draw a big circle around the perimeter of the hoop. You want it to be larger than the ring so you can pull it tight and center the plaid to your liking. Excess is fine since we can trim it off.

Place the cut fabric on top of the small hoop

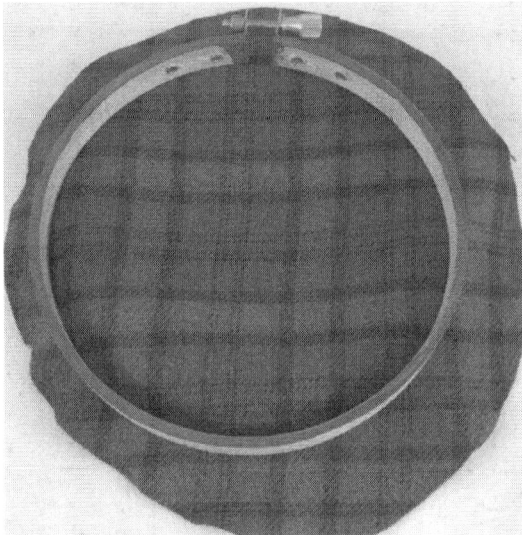

Next set the top hoop into place.

Now is the time for pattern placement if you wish to center the plaid a certain way

Trim the excess from the back. Notice the painted areas of the small hoop visible on the back

Finally used the E6000 to glue on the Christmas picks to the front. selected Christmas picks and apparently lots of other folks do too because Hobby Lobby has two whole rows of them to select from!

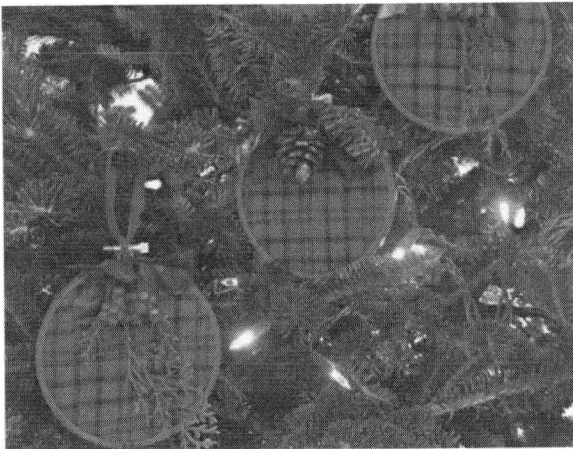

'Merry Christmas' Word Embroidery Hoop

you'll need:

- free Christmas ornament embroidery pattern

- 3 inch embroidery hoop

- embroidery floss (DMC colors: 501, 562, 966, 817, and 3799)

- felt for backing

- small ribbon

Instructions:

1. Transfer your design onto the black fabric.

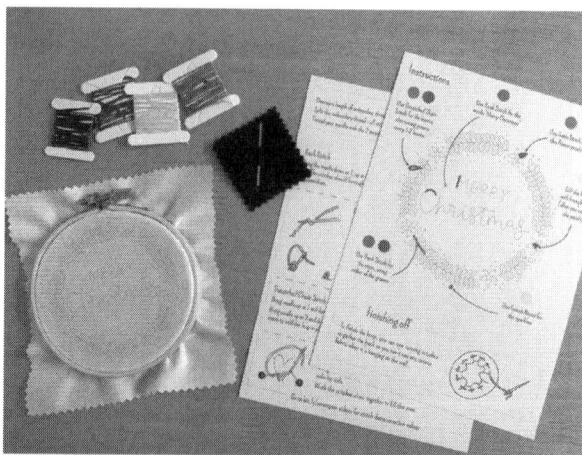

2. Stitch all outlines as the photo shows with a back stitch. Reference the photo for color choice. Use 3 strands of floss for all stitches.

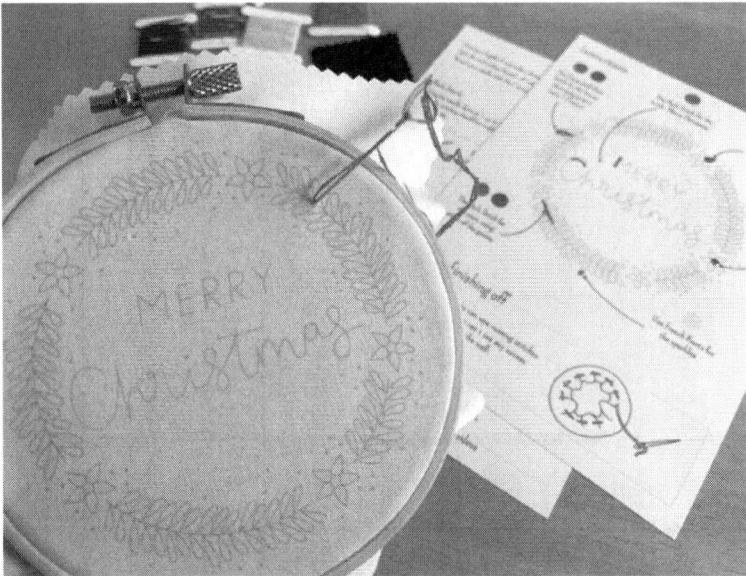

3. Fill letters with a sketchy looking satin stitch, leaving some spaces to give it that "chalk" look.
4. Scatter french knots around the design for a few snowflakes.

5. Finish hoop by trimming fabric on back side to 1/2". Hot glue fabric to the back inside of the hoop. Glue pom pom trim around the back edge of the hoop so the pom poms stand out from the hoop. Glue a piece of felt over the back of the hoop to finish off.

Elf Mini Hoop Christmas Ornaments

Materials:

- 10" square of fabric (if you want to stitch them in the same hoop. Otherwise two 5" squares) for background
- Aurifil Floss – Red, Gray, Green and Yellow
- Wool Blend felt in Yellow, Green and Gray
- Small Red Pom Pom Trim
- Larger White Pom Pom Trim
- HeatnBond Fusible Webbing
- Ribbon for hanging
- Glue
- Marking Pen
- Two 3" Embroidery Hoops
- One 8" Embroidery Hoop
- Elf Hoop Ornament Patterns

21

Begin by cutting out the patterns and arranging them so you can fit them both in an 8" hoop, with plenty of space for trimming around the circles in between them. Mark the designs onto the background fabric for the lettering.

Cut out squares of wool felt slightly larger than the pattern shapes. Iron pieces of fusible webbing to one side and cut out the shapes. Iron the felt pieces in place according to the pattern. It might help to iron them on the front, then flip the fabric over and iron on the wrong side as well, since it's sometimes a little hard to get the felt to fuse in place because of the thickness.

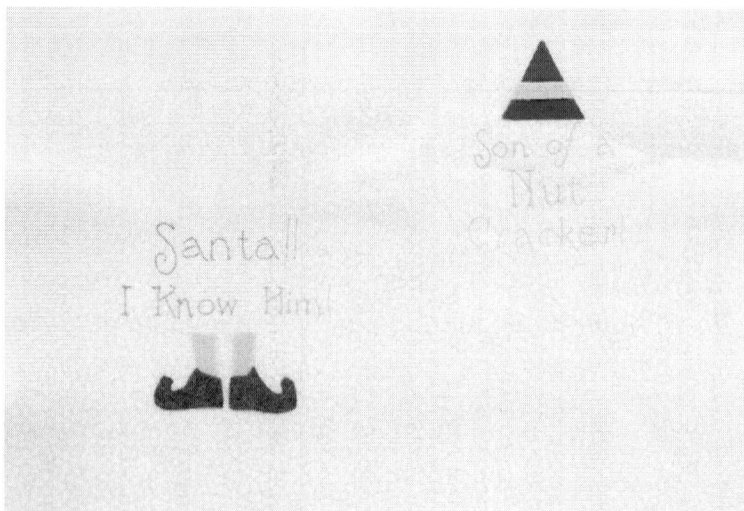

Embroider the lettering with small back stitches in red floss. Stitch down the felt shapes with small running stitches in coordinating floss colors. Embroidery the little feather on the hat with small satin stitches.

Take the fabric out of the larger hoop and place one of the designs in the 3" hoop. Trim closely around the outer edge of the hoop, just enough so you can glue the fabric to the back side of the hoop. Repeat with the other design. Glue the fabrics to the back of the hoops.

If you want to add on the two layers of pom pom trim, glue the small red trim around the outer edge of the hoop. I found this trim at Hobby Lobby but I think most fabric stores are carrying the small pom pom trim as well.

Repeat with the larger white trim, layering the edge of the white pom pom trim on top of the red.

Embroidery Hoop Christmas Ornaments

Add your ribbons for tying and show off your cute new ornaments!

Snowflake Embroidery Pattern Tutorial

You Will Need…

- Embroidery Hoop

- Fabric big enough to fit the hoop for a stand-alone project, or the item you wish to embroider.

- Embroidery Floss in the color of your choice. If you are embroidering your snowflakes on dark fabric choose a bright white or pale blue. If you are using white fabric like in the photos shown here, try a light blue or silver floss instead. Don't be afraid to use more than one color in your snowflakes. Pro tip: metallic floss makes for fun & festive embroidery snowflakes!

- Free Snowflake Embroidery Pattern: Download and resize however you like. Pattern transfer instructions are included in the PDF.

- Sewing Scissors, a Water Soluble Marking Pen and maybe a Small Ruler to keep your stitches straight.

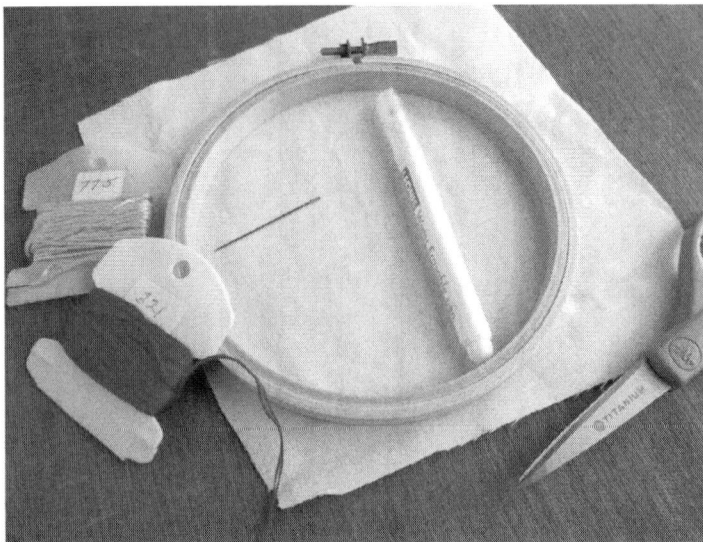

Snowflake Embroidery Pattern #1

Embroidery Hoop Christmas Ornaments

Let's start with the most basic snowflake, designed this one to be simple and easily stitchable in even the smallest size. The only stitch required is back stitch. If you are not familiar with this stitch, or you need a refresher, be sure to visit my Basic Embroidery Stitches tutorial. For this snowflake, chosen to use two contrasting colors of embroidery floss. The bright red (DMC 321) will create the long lines while the pale blue (DMC 775) is used for the short, diagonal lines.

Thread your needle with floss. For this size snowflake, I'm using 4 strands of DMC floss. Using back stitch, make a single stitch along the first line. Continue stitching until you reach the end of the line.

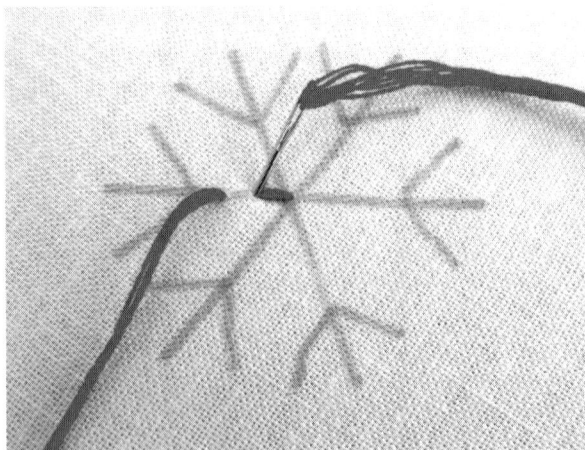

For this size snowflake, using five stitches on each line – three below the slanted V and two above. Depending on the size snowflake you are stitching you might want to adjust the stitch count and length. This is also where the mini ruler comes in. If you're a stickler for details and want to be sure each stitch is even, measure and mark the fabric ahead of time. Or, if you're like me and don't mind a few imperfections, go ahead and eyeball it.

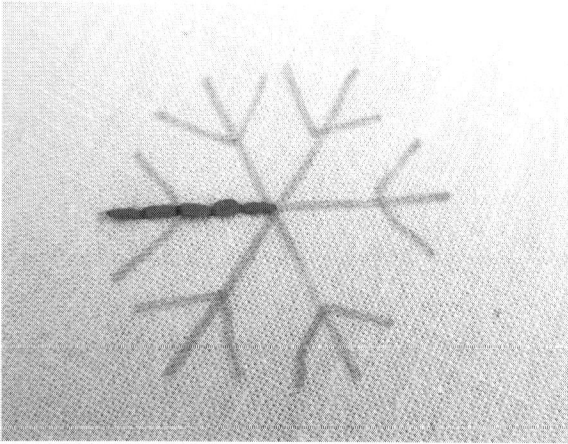

Once you've completed the first line, flip the fabric over and weave your thread down to the middle of the snowflake. Come back up on the next line and stitch to the end. Continue this process until all the long lines are filled in.

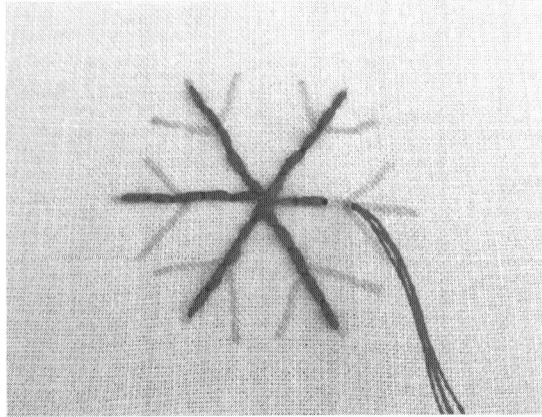

If you are using a second color, end the first floss on the back and re-thread the needle, using four strands of DMC floss in pale blue (DMC 775). Start in the middle of one of the short diagonal lines and fill in with two stitches on each line. End the first stitch in the middle of the third and fourth stitch of the long line. Again, depending on the size of your snowflakes you might need to adjust the stitch count and size.

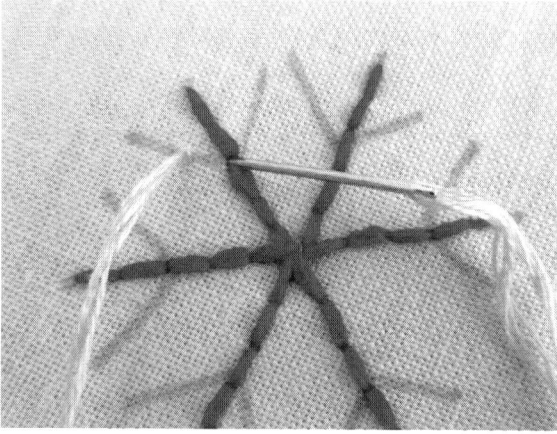

Move over to the adjacent diagonal line and repeat.

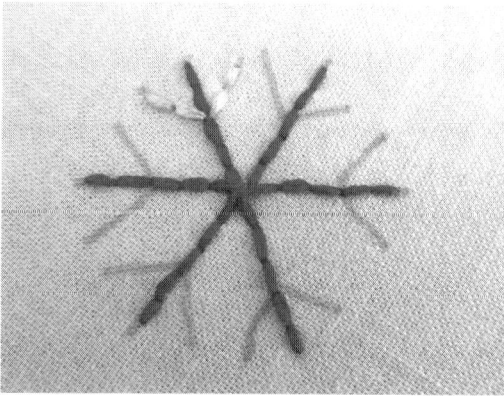

Continue around the snowflake until all the lines are stitched and you

have a beautiful snowflake!

Snowflake Embroidery Pattern #2

Now that we've learned the basics, let's move on to the second snowflake pattern. For this one, using four strands of a single color floss (DMC 775). Feel free to add more colors to your liking. Once again, the only stitch required is back stitch. Begin by making a single back stitch at the end of one of the long lines. Start the stitch at the intersection of the two short diagonal lines and end it at the top of the long line.

Make three more stitches to complete the section. Start in the middle and stitch outward.

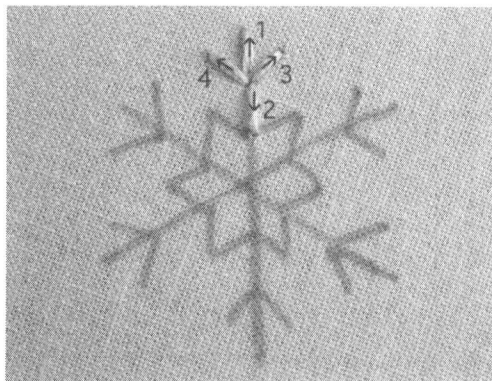

Flip your work over, weave the floss through until it reaches the bottom of the #2 stitch. Take the floss back up through the fabric at the middle point to the right. Make a single back stitch.

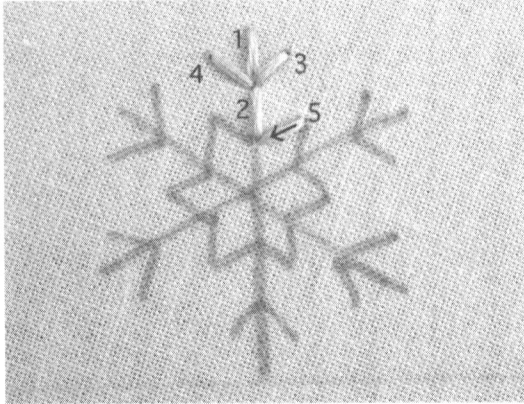

Now, simply continue around the snowflake in the same fashion making sure that each stitch begins where the last one ends.

Finish off the snowflake by filling in the center spokes with single back stitches.

Tada! Look at that beauty!

Snowflake Embroidery Pattern #3

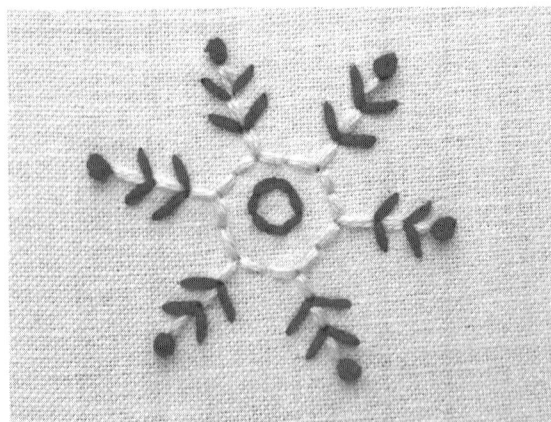

The third and final snowflake embroidery pattern is the most detailed. While it looks complicated it's actually quite easy and only requires one additional stitch along with back stitch. For this snowflake, used 4 strands each of light blue (DMC 775) and bright red (DMC 321). Feel free to use a single color or go wild and choose three or four!

Starting with the light blue floss, back stitch around the inner hexagon shape. For this size snowflake, using two stitches per side. Adjust as necessary according to the size of your snowflake.

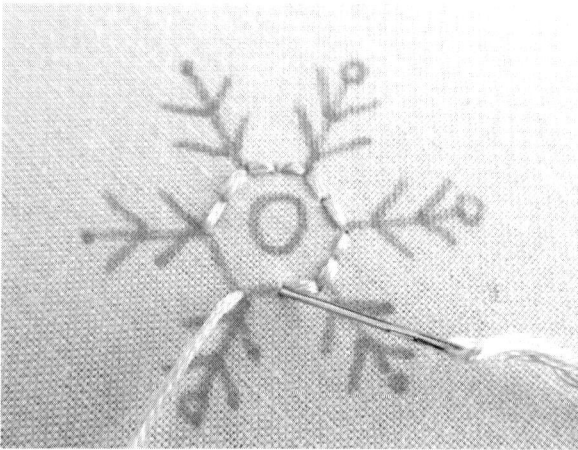

After completing the middle, back stitch up each long line. Remember to weave the floss through the back before starting each line. This is especially important if you are stitching with a dark floss on a light fabric.

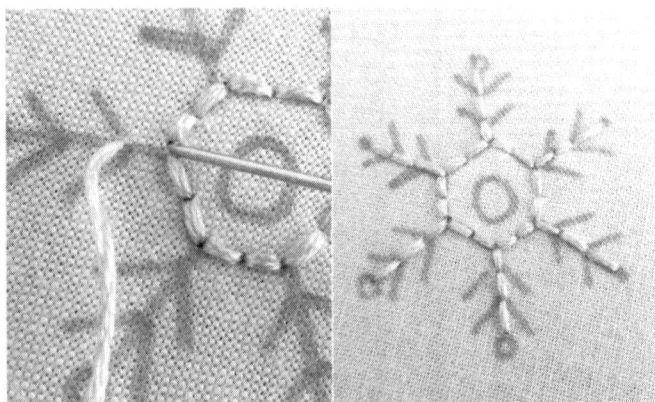

If you are using a second color floss, end the first color on the back and thread the needle with the new color. Starting at the bottom of a long line, work your way back and forth on the diagonal lines with single back stitches.

At the top of the line make a single french knot. Bring the needle to the front of the fabric and wrap the thread once or twice around the needle. Holding the thread with one hand, push the needle back through the fabric directly next to the where you came out. Gently pull the needle through to form a complete knot. For more detailed instructions, take a look at my French Knot Embroidery Tutorial.

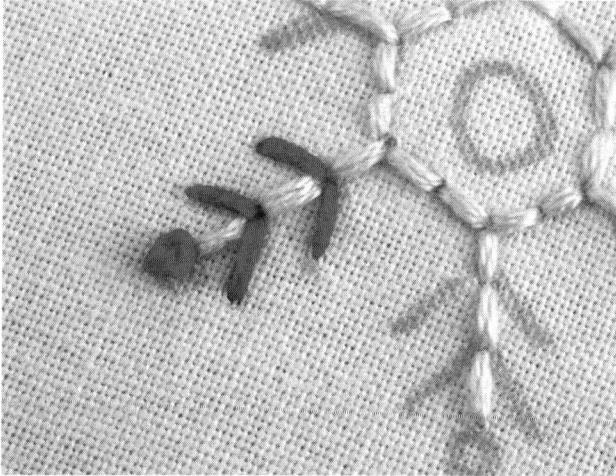

Work all the way around the snowflake, filling in the short diagonal lines with back stitch and adding a small french knot to the end of each long line.

41

Finally, stitch the inner circle. You could fill it in with a cluster of french knots, or follow my lead and simply stitch around the edge with back stitch.

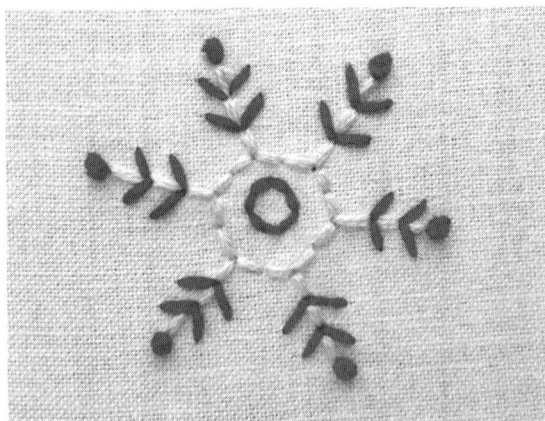

Put Your Snowflake Embroidery Skills to Use!

Santa Hat Embroidery Ornament

Supplies:

- Ultra Punch Needle Set + threader
- Locking plastic embroidery hoop
- Cotton twill fabric
- Santa Hat Pattern
- Pencil
- Red & white embroidery floss
- 3 inch wooden embroidery hoop
- Scissors
- Hot glue gun

Embroidery Hoop Christmas Ornaments

Instructions:

1. Download and print this Santa Hat Pattern. The circle around the hat should be 3 inches wide

2. Hold the pattern against a window and place your fabric over the top, lightly trace the hat with a pencil. Make sure you leave enough room to hoop the design

3. Tightly hoop the fabric in the plastic hoop

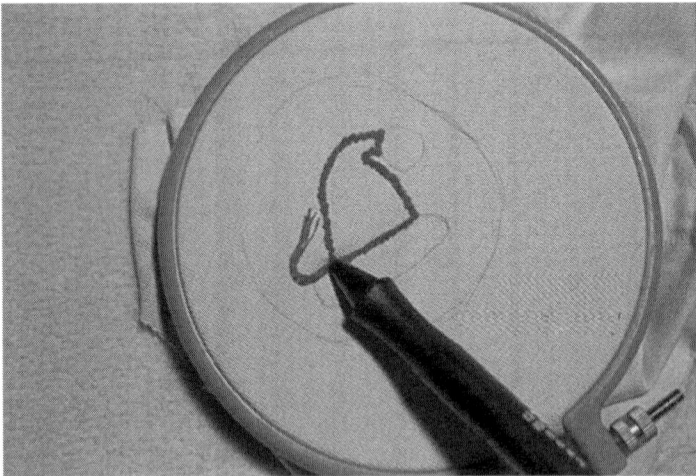

4. Begin with the red thread, set the needle to a length of 3 or 4 and punch the body of the hat starting with the outline and working

inwards

5. Switch to the white thread and change the needle length to a 7 or
8. Punch the brim and ball on the hat
6. When you're done flip it over and check for any empty spaces, fill them in if you find some
7. Unhoop and clip any extra long loops that stick out
8. Place the bottom of the wooden hoop on the table, lay the fabric over it with the right side up
9. Sandwich it together by sliding on the top hoop, make sure to keep the thumb screw at the top so you have a way to hang the ornament when it's done. Tighten the hoop
10. Cut off the excess fabric leaving about 1/2 inch

11. Flip over the hoop and hot glue around the hoop, folding the excess fabric into the glue

12. Braid three strands of floss together and tie off the ends, fold it in half and pull the loop through the hole under the thumb screw for the embroidery floss. Pull the ends of the braid through the loop and pull tight.

A Christmas Story Leg Lamp Ornament

Materials:

- 4" embroidery hoop
- 6" piece of white background fabric
- Small fabric scraps – gray, black, and light yellow
- Mustard or Gold Wool/Wool Blend Felt
- DMC Black Embroidery Floss – 310
- Marking Pen
- Coordinating trim for Edge
- Ribbon
- 4" circle of felt for backing
- Hot Glue
- HeatnBond Fusible Adhesive
- Leg Lamp Ornament Pattern

Embroidery Hoop Christmas Ornaments

Start by cutting out your pattern pieces. Iron fusible adhesive to the wrong sides of the fabric and felt scraps and cut out your pattern pieces for the lampshade, leg, shoe and base. Transfer the words to the background fabric with a marking pen.

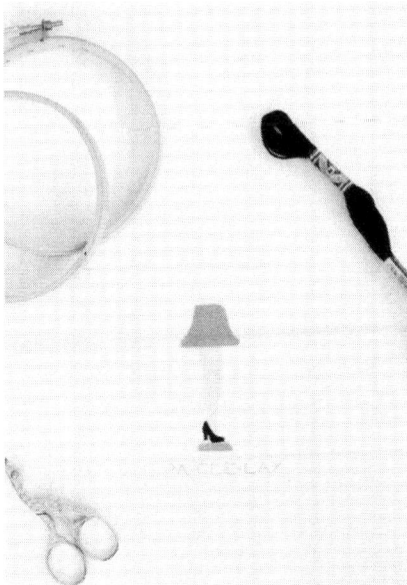

Embroider the lettering with 3 strands of floss using a back stitch. Use one strand of floss for everything else. Stitch small outlines on the base. Stitch diagonal lines across the leg for the stockings, along with 3 strands of horizontal floss just under the lampshade for the top of the stocking. Stitch detail lines on the lampshade, following the pattern lines. Stitch small lines of fringe all along the bottom of the lampshade.

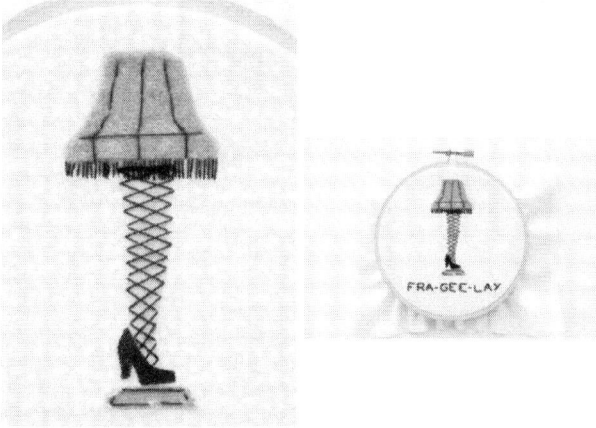

Finish the hoop by trimming the fabric to about 1/2 inch and gluing it to the back inside edge. Glue your trim around the outside and finish the back by gluing a 4" circle of felt over the back of the hoop. Add a small length of ribbon to hang the ornament with!

Here are some other ornaments from Ornament

Printed in Great Britain
by Amazon

66595111R00031